A Review of the Book

DARK AGENDA

The War to Destroy Christian America

by David Horowitz

Introduction by
State Rep. Gary Giordano (1985–89)

Book Review by
Professor Kevin Peterson (Major, USAF, Ret.)
National Project Director, Conservative Christian Center

What They're Saying
about *A Review of the Book Dark Agenda:*
The War to Destroy Christian America

The children of light must register to vote, learn more about our adversary, vote their conscience and speak out more often in the public policy process, so that good people will win elections and vanquish those who follow this *Dark Agenda*. Or as Lincoln worried, we'll perish from the face of the earth.

State Rep. Gary Giordano (1985–89)

Conservative minded, church-going Christians need to stop listening to the excuses of politicians who claim to be with us but won't speak out and act on the issues of importance to us. This review of *Dark Agenda* helps document the work of those who hate us and work to destroy the America we know and love. A call to arms.

William E. Saracino
Executive Vice President, White House Watch Fund
Former Political Director, Draft Ben Carson for President
Former 2020 GOP Convention Delegate pledged to Donald Trump

Those who hate people of faith have, since the Obama years, infiltrated our military to do their version of an anti-Christian, ethnic cleansing. *A Review of the Book Dark Agenda: the War to Destroy Christian America*, for the first time, really explains who are these people, and why they hate us. Most important, it is a wake up call. Thank you to Conservative Christian Center for publishing this, and we pray your readers will respond generously to your call for help.

Lt. Col. Dennis Gillem, USA (Ret.)
Chairman, Veterans Advisory Board of Uniformed Services League
Host of the nationally syndicated Frontlines of Freedom Radio Show

If you go to Church but you are not registered to vote… if you are a good Christian who did not vote… if you are with us on the public policy issues which divide liberals from conservatives… this *Review of the Book Dark Agenda: The War to Destroy Christian America* is for you. We need to increase our numbers and our influence, especially with seniors who are believers. This handy pocketbook helps you understand what we are up against and why we need you with us.

Ronald Wilcox
Executive Director, SecureAmerica Alliance, Former 2020 GOP Convention Delegate pledged to Donald Trump

If you don't help, then the bad people with their dreadful, anti-Christian, anti-America philosophy, will not only win elections and run the country—but they will implement their *Dark Agenda*. The choice is yours.

By Ross Cleveland
South Central PA Coordinator, Conservative Christian Center

We've been working in south central PA for 10 years to increase voter turnout among church-going people of faith. This *Review of the Book Dark Agenda: The War to Destroy Christian America*, will be a big help to our local clubs. Thank you to our national organization the Conservative Christian Center for providing this great tool for us. I hope that readers of this short Book Review will go right out and buy the David Horowitz book.

Emy Delgaudio
Chairman, York County Chapter, Conservative Christian Center

Now we get to the root cause of the left's hatred of President Trump and his followers. The defenders of our Judeo-Christian culture can now see who these people are, and what motivates their work to destroy us. Most important, it helps church-going people of faith understand why they must be far more active in political and public policy questions for this Republic to survive.

Owen Jones
National Spokesman, Americans for a Conservative Agenda
formerly Americans for the Trump Agenda

A Review of the Book Dark Agenda: The War to Destroy Christian America, is published by FreedomPublishers.com for Conservative Christian Center.

This is a Review, not the full book. Freedom Publishers is not associated with David Horowitz or the publisher of his book, which we recommend and which can be purchased at FreedomPublishers.com, Amazon.com, Barnes and Noble or your local bookstore.

Book Review by Professor Kevin Peterson, Major, USAF (Ret.), Project Director, Conservative Christian Center.

Special thanks to the following who have made the publishing of this review possible:

    Senior Editor: Owen Jones

    Executive Editor: Hanover Henry

    Cover design and typesetting: Spencer Grahl

    Legal Counsel: Amanda G. Hyland, Esq.
    Taylor, English, Duma LLP, Atlanta, Georgia

This publication was made possible thanks to a grant from the Freedom Center Foundation.

This pocketbook and the organizations which have worked together to publish and circulate it do not advocate for or against candidates for local, state or federal office

Donations to pay for more copies of this pocketbook to be printed and distributed may be made to:

Conservative Christian Center
A project of United States Public Policy Council, a 501(c)4 public policy corporation. Donations not tax deductible.

ConservativeChristianCenter.org

or mail

Conservative Christian Center
Freedom Center, P.O. Box 820
Stuarts Draft, VA 24477-0820.

or

Freedom Center Foundation
Chairman@FreedomCenterFoundation.org

Gifts to the Foundation are tax deductible on your federal tax return. Gifts of $1000 or more only please. Recognized by IRS as a 501(c)3 charity.

Additional copies of this pocketbook may be ordered for a gift of $5 each, 3 for $10, 10 for $20, 100 for $150 plus postage and handling of $3 plus 10%. Inquire for larger orders. Info@ConservativeChristianCenter.org

FreedomPublishers.org for online orders and other books and pocketbooks including the full size book, *Dark Agenda: The War to Destroy Christian America* by David Horowitz.

Introduction
By former State Representative Gary Giordano

It may seem odd to introduce a book about the war to destroy Christian America, by citing the ancient Chinese general, Sun Tzu. Perhaps his most famous saying, written many years before the birth of Christ, is "know your enemy."

Sadly, too many church-going people of faith aren't aware that there is a war underway against them, a war to destroy even the knowledge that America was formed by Christians whose ideas for government came about because of their belief in the traditional, Judeo-Christian worldview.

And even among many who know about this war to obliterate the Christian roots of American freedom, most are not aware, as the book we will review here documents, that their enemy is atheistic, Christian-hating Marxists, whether they call themselves today's justice warriors or admit to their Marxist heritage.

In *Dark Agenda: the War to Destroy Christian America*, David Horowitz explains and documents who is behind this war and what motivates their hatred of Christians and all things connected to God—including his followers in America.

Horowitz should know. He was raised in a household by such people, who trained him to follow in their Marxist, hate-America footsteps. As a revolutionary, he did them proud, becoming the editor of the largest anti-America, leftwing publication of his time, *Ramparts*.

Let me be very clear. I don't cite Sun Tzu and his "know your enemy" statement in order to suggest that we should be friends with those who would destroy the freedoms that most Americans take for granted.

And I do not cite "know your enemy" as an exercise in passive resistance to the anti-America revolution today's followers of President Joe Biden and cultural Marxism propose.

My purpose, in this introduction and my endorsement of this splendid book by David Horowitz, is to join him and the Conservative Christian Center, in sounding the alarm to church-going people of faith in America.

Your most cherished beliefs and principles

are under attack. The enemy and his goals are defined clearly in this book, so appropriately named, *Dark Agenda*.

God is light. The enemy of darkness. And which always vanquishes darkness when the light is raised up. This idea is repeated often throughout the Bible.

America's founders were strong believers in the Judeo-Christian worldview. In their Declaration of Independence and later their Constitution, it was their Christian worldview which raised up the Light for all to see.

Those beliefs—especially the idea that we are creations of a loving Almighty God who endowed us with inalienable rights, are under assault as never before since the Founding of this great Republic. They are going to vanish unless we work together to defend them.

The children of light must register to vote, learn more about our adversary, vote their conscience and speak out more often in the public policy process, so that good people will win elections and vanquish those who follow this *Dark Agenda*. Or as Lincoln worried, we'll perish from the face of the earth.

1. Overview

This book is written explicitly as a wake-up call to American Christians, especially patriotic ones. People who are devout believers in Biblical and Church teachings and appreciate the fact that America was founded on the principle of religious liberty. Ironically, it is written by an agnostic Jew, David Horowitz. He is calling on American Christians to become more aware of how rapidly we are losing our religious liberties, and why. In essence, it is a call to action, as the author believes Christians can become more aware of and more effective in defeating the "Dark Agenda" of America's cultural Marxists.

It is not a religious book, or even less a theological treatise, but Horowitz has a better understanding than most, of the role played by the Christian religion, in shaping and molding our nation from the very beginning. He articulates the essential principles of Christian theology as they relate to human nature and its fundamental principles better than many

Christians. He employs that understanding to expose the fundamental flaws of Marxism and any type of political ideology that promises a utopian future.

For too long, religious conservatives and traditional believers assumed that Marxism could not and will never take hold in America. They were wrong. Marxists have taken over most of our national institutions, including the Democrat Party. There is a long history leading up to this condition which David Horowitz documents clearly and effectively. He knows whereof he speaks, having been raised by devout Marxists and present at the creation of some of the most effective Marxist organizations in the 1960's, including Students for A Democratic Society (SDS) and the Black Panthers and as Editor of the nation's largest "New Left" magazine, *Ramparts*.

He began to question all of his political positions when the Black Panthers murdered one of his best friends, and in so doing revealed to him the truth: Marxism is a movement of criminal thugs, not the idealistic reform movement he thought it was.

To some readers, the information in this extremely valuable and relevant book will be old news. Even so, it will come as a shock to most Christians just how deeply embedded Marxism has become in American institutions, going back at least a hundred years.

Perhaps Horowitz's most important revelations involve the idea of *issue framing*, and just how it works.

He warns that Christians may no longer delude themselves into a sympathetic adoption of the latest issue just because it sounds good, like being against injustice or oppression—things that devout and sincere Christians have always opposed. As the 1960's radical SDS publication *New Left Notes* put it: **"The issue is never the issue. The issue is always the revolution."** [emphasis added]

This very effective issue framing is the reason why the Hard Left cultural Marxists have won virtually every major cultural battle in America since the early 1960's, from abortion to same sex marriage to the latest accusation that America is a systemically racist nation. The only major cultural battle the cultural Marxists lost was the battle for the Equal Rights Amendment to the Constitution. They only lost because they got out-organized at the very last minute by Phyllis Schlafly who saw it for what it really was: A Marxist attempt to erase any distinction between the sexes and destroy the family.

The ERA was right out of the Communist Manifesto with its goal of destroying freedom as we know it in the United States. This truth has never been acknowledged by its supporters in the Democrat Party and the media, nor admitted to by the Marxist leadership cadre who organized and led the nationwide campaign to persuade the states to approve their Constitutional Amendment.

2. Atheism and Hatred Toward Christians

"The New Atheists" are a cohort of scientists and thought leaders who have strayed into intellectual territory—holding themselves out as experts—which they actually know little or nothing about: religion and theology. Prominent among them are the authors of a manifesto published in 2006 called "The God Delusion." This manifesto "maintains that post-Darwinian scientific advances have rendered any belief in God irrational and unnecessary," says Horowitz.

Evolutionary biologist Richard Dawkins is their most prominent spokesman. He views religious teachings as "crude and fallacy-ridden attempts to provide nonscientific accounts of natural forces and phenomena," writes Horowitz. Dawkins' conclusions are based on the false assumption Christians read the Bible only as a historically literal and scientific account and not for its more important underlying spiritual truths. Dawkins completely "dismisses the more important moral and spiritual dimensions of religion," writes Horowitz.

The most important aspect of Dawkins' argument, according to Horowitz, is "the unscientific *animus* with which it is pursued." Dawkins describes the God of the Old and New Testament as "arguably the most unpleasant character in all of fiction: jealous and proud of it; a petty, unjust, unforgiving control freak; a vindictive, bloodthirsty ethnic cleanser; a misogynistic, homophobic, racist, infanticidal, genocidal, filicidal, pestilential, megalomaniacal, sadomasochistic, capriciously malevolent bully."

Horowitz dissects these accusations with common sense arguments. More to the point is the accusation by Dawkins and the New Atheists that all religious people are just stupid. Other contemporary scientists such as Dr. Francis Collins, who headed the Human Genome Project, have taken on Dawkins in public debates, defending both belief in God as well as the contributions of religion and religious people to society.

But as Horowitz points out, the hatred and loathing toward religious people by the New

Atheists is caused by the fact that traditional religion is an obstacle to their new religion. "They see themselves as liberators and pioneers of a new millennium for the human race. They envision a future in which religion has been vanquished and rationality prevails," writes Horowitz. They are convinced science will transform human nature and bring about a utopian age governed by "reason, enlightenment, and social justice."

This vision of an earthly redemption is a fantasy, says Horowitz, "in which human beings aspire to act as gods and create a new world." It's nothing new. It is the faith of Marxists and Communists who set out to liberate us all from "original sin." It is the temptation of Satan, says Horowitz, who tempted the first man and woman, saying, "Then your eyes shall be opened and ye shall be as gods." And it is "the cause of the monstrous catastrophes of the twentieth century which were engineered by socialists in Germany and the Communist block."

3. Horowitz's Personal Story

David Horowitz's personal pilgrimage away from Marxism is a powerful witness, even if he still refers to himself as an "agnostic." He grew up in a hard-core Marxist family who celebrated the Jewish holidays marking freedom from oppression: Chanukah and Passover. They refused to participate in the holidays that were about "the state of individual souls." His family did not care about individual souls, only "the salvation of mankind," he writes. "We wanted justice for oppressed classes and races, and we looked at synagogues as reactionary institutions—houses of superstition whose prayers and preaching served to keep the oppressed in line."

Horowitz came to the realization this atheistic creed was a religion itself. The progressive god was history which was inexorably marching "to a promised land." Most disturbing to him was the destructive fantasy that led his parents "into supporting an empire whose rulers murdered millions" (The Soviet Union).

Horowitz recognized progressivist and Marxist politics as a derivation of the ancient Christian heresy called Pelagianism. Pelagius believed human beings were naturally good, but society lead them down paths which are bad. Pelagius taught "sins were acts *against* human nature," and not a consequence of human nature. If enough Christians could resist the temptations of this world, "they could achieve an earthly paradise—and they could achieve this paradise without help from God," Horowitz writes.

This is no different than Marxism, except Marxists remove God from the world entirely. Instead, Horowitz now recognizes man has been given free will. "Free will gives each individual the power to do good—or evil. Free will makes us the authors of our own choices, our own sins, our own fates—not other people, not classes or races or genders."

What was the shock that led Horowitz to this revelation? The Black Panthers murdered his friend, Betty Van Patter. She was a "kindhearted leftist" who kept the Black Panthers' books. When she discovered the Black Panthers were engaged in financial fraud, they killed her to keep her quiet.

Remarkably, and those of you who are believing Christians would recognize this as a revelation from God, Horowitz understood in a flash that good and evil are not social constructs. Injustice is "the result of human selfishness, deceitfulness, malice, envy, greed, and lust."

"The social redeemers view the Christian concern for the salvation of individual souls as counterrevolutionary, a cause of social oppression. To them, religious believers are obstacles on the path to the future—**and must be removed**." [emphasis added]

This book documents the many blatant attempts by cultural Marxists to eliminate any and all Christian influence in politics and society. If you are a believer, then you must be "removed," because you stand athwart their history.

4. The Most Influential Cultural Marxist in American History

Most people who have been engaged in the pro-life movement are familiar with the name Margaret Sanger. They know her to be an advocate of racist eugenics. Eugenics is the theory espousing that human beings should be treated as livestock. Inferior traits should be forcefully bred out of the gene pool, and superior traits should be forcefully bred into the gene pool in order to produce a superior race of people. Many prominent Americans of her day were also eugenicists, including Presidents Theodore Roosevelt and Woodrow Wilson, as well as industrialist Henry Ford.

What most people are not aware of are Sanger's deep roots in the cultural Marxist movement. While Horowitz does not explicitly define cultural Marxism in this book, it is important to point out Marx never successfully defined economic Marxism. The central agenda of the *Communist Manifesto* was cultural: to eliminate any vestige of Christian and bourgeois morality, to eliminate families and make procreation exclusively a state project in order to engineer a perfect society. Economic Marxism has failed miserably. Even Marxists recognize that fact. Which is why cultural Marxism has become the central focus of the left.

Margaret Sanger was early in the game. She was associated with the creation of the American Civil Liberties Union, which was founded for the purpose of bringing about a Marxist society. Its most prominent figure was Emma Goldman, known as "Red Emma." "Goldman was a revolutionary who plotted with her lover to assassinate Henry Clay Frick, Chairman of the Carnegie Steel Company," writes Horowitz. When the plot failed, she was deported to the Soviet Union!

Sanger was closely associated with Goldman. Sanger was first and foremost a revolutionary, "openly proclaiming that birth control was the means by which she intended to change the world," writes Horowitz. She not only promoted contraception "but moral and political anarchy," he writes. She authored a monthly newspaper, "Woman Rebel." Its motto? "No gods, no masters!" Sanger wrote: "The rebel woman claims the right to be an unmarried mother." She asserted that women have a duty to face the world "with a go-to-hell look in the eyes; to have an ideal; to speak and act in defiance of convention."

In a profile published in *The New Yorker*, Sanger was quoted as writing: "A Defense of Assassination," "The Song of the Bomb," and an editorial declaring: "Even if dynamite were to serve no other purpose than to call forth the spirit of revolutionary solidarity, it would prove its great value."

Sanger believed the world's problems—poverty, hunger, war—stemmed from the "fit" having too few children and the "unfit" having too many. Planned Parenthood was founded out of this violent, revolutionary, totalitarian rhetoric. The rest is history. Through lies and deceit, Planned Parenthood managed to manipulate a willing Supreme Court into abolishing laws against contraception, and it was only one logical legal step from there to overturning anti-abortion laws throughout America. Since then, there have been over

65 million surgical abortions in the U.S., with 40% of those abortions being black babies! That not only represents 26 million more black people who would have been alive today without abortion, but also the children and grandchildren of those 26 million black babies, who are intentionally targeted, year after year, by Planned Parenthood "clinics."

With Margaret Sanger there never was any interest in or compassion for unwed mothers. Nor has that ever been a motivating factor for the leadership and supporters of Planned Parenthood. According to Horowitz, the issue was and is and always has been **violent Marxist revolution. That's the only issue**. Yet the cultural Marxists continue to successfully frame the "issue" of abortion in terms of compassion for women with unwanted pregnancies, or more broadly speaking, "women's health." Note once again the issue framing tactic.

5. Two Other Case Studies in Marxist Issue Framing That Have Led to Disastrous Consequences

Horowitz explores several other "issues" that were all started by an intensely dedicated group of Marxists. For example, the "gay rights movement" was intentionally founded and organized by men who believed that having sex with strangers, and as many strangers as possible, was a revolutionary act. The Gay Liberation Front took its name from the Vietnamese National Liberation Front (NLF), the official name of the Vietnamese Communist Viet Cong. In the view of gay radicals, "existing sexual prohibitions reflected no lessons drawn from humanity's biological realities and moral experience; they were merely 'social constructions' imposed by an oppressive culture," writes Horowitz.

The effect of this radical agenda was immediate and devastating. By encouraging promiscuous sex among hundreds, even thousands of strangers, the leaders of the "gay rights" movement caused massive outbreaks of diseases, long before the initial outbreak of AIDS. Public health officials who tried to address the problem were attacked, vilified and condemned as "homophobic," a form of "racist" prejudice against gays.

The cultural Marxist founders of the "gay rights" movement cleverly couched their demands in the same terms as the civil rights movement, without explaining what a man who is having sex with hundreds or thousands of strangers has to do with prejudice against black people. As a result, according to Horowitz, public officials were politically pressured into licensing "bathhouses," and even turned a blind eye toward public sex activity.

Horowitz writes about one "gay" theorist at NYU, Michael Warner, who explained: "The phenomenology of a sex club encounter is an experience of *world making*." Note the familiar Marxist language. Christians and religious people have failed to improve the world. They are the real oppressors. We are here to remake the world—in our own image.

Horowitz quotes the author of *The Joy of Gay*

Sex who proposed "gay men should wear their sexually transmitted diseases like red badges of courage in a war against a sex-negative society." Then came AIDS.

The cultural Marxists behind the "gay rights" movement opposed any efforts to take precautions against the spread of AIDS as well, including testing and contact tracing and the use of condoms, condemning them as "homophobic." They pressured the government to describe AIDS as "an equal opportunity virus," which it most certainly is not.

Horowitz argues persuasively that the more than 500,000 deaths from AIDS "were entirely preventable if the public health system had not been crippled by radical ideologues." This book was published in 2018. Had it been published in 2021, I'm confident that Horowitz would have found ample examples of how leftist ideology contributed significantly to the Covid death toll as well.

Another disastrous example of the influence of cultural Marxism is the Supreme Court decision banning God from public education (Madeleine Murray was a member of the

Socialist Labor Party). Once again, he provides ample documentation.

Please read the book for yourself so that you may develop the awareness to recognize the **issue framing** at which the cultural Marxists are so good. Christians should never fall for the trap of agreeing with a cultural Marxist just because they have figured out how to sound compassionate in public or effectively leverage flowery rhetoric.

When you read this book, which we strongly recommend, you will be trained to recognize the next "issue." These days it seems there is a new one each month. But there is little doubt that Margaret Sanger's pathbreaking, in your face, violent revolutionary Marxism in defense of murdering millions of innocent, defenseless babies has been the most destructive force in American history, in many ways the precursor to all of the other cultural Marxist "issues,"

6. Barack Hussein Obama

We all remember President Obama as a liberal, even a leftist, president. What many people do not know, and a fact which Horowitz exposes in this book, is the degree to which Obama deliberately pursued anti-Christian policies.

A month after Obama's inauguration, the founder of the Military Religious Freedom Foundation, Michael Weinstein, was able to gain an audience with a member of the Joint Chiefs of Staff—Air Force General Norton A. Schwartz. As the direct result of Weinstein's influence with the Pentagon during the Obama years, "religious expression in the military became a criminal offense," writes Horowitz. His foundation has nothing to do with religious freedom. In fact, Horowitz describes it as "an anti-Christian hate group."

"Weinstein made the case to the Pentagon that Christians in the military—including chaplains—who shared their beliefs with others were committing 'treason' and 'spiritual rape,'" writes Horowitz. "Under President

Obama, the Pentagon adopted Weinstein's false view that the First Amendment was an anti-religious stricture."

A significant part of this book contains Horowitz's review of America's Founding as primarily and essentially for the purpose of protecting religious liberty. Oddly, the cultural Marxists claim the First Amendment does not permit Americans to be religious!

As President, Obama also notably exploited identity politics to "fundamentally transform the United States of America." This agenda began with the misnamed "Affordable Care Act."

This act was an assault on individual freedom. Obama lied about that as well as other aspects of his proposal. The author of the plan, Jonathan Gruber, explained why he, Obama and all of the supporters of "Obamacare" had to lie: "If you made it explicit that healthy people pay in and sick people get money, it would not have passed, okay? Lack of transparency is a huge political advantagee…."

Not only did Obama lie about the economics of the ACA, he covered up the extent of its anti-Christian agenda. Horowitz describes the

ACA as "a dagger aimed at the heart of the First Amendment—and the ability of the American people to form their own communities of belief."

The Obama Administration immediately began an assault on the Little Sisters of the Poor, who could not, as a matter of religious conscience, comply with the Obamacare mandates to provide abortion inducing drugs and contraceptives under their healthplan. Failure to comply meant millions of dollars in fines. To begin to appreciate the utter insanity and Orwellian nature of the Obama Administration's war against the Little Sisters of the Poor, it's necessary to point out that they only served elderly women!

The Little Sisters of the Poor went to court. As the appeals process progressed, "the nuns' belief in the 'sanctity of life' was attacked by feminists as an unconstitutional discrimination against women," writes Horowitz. "The Little Sisters were putting an 'undue burden' on women and were therefore part of the oppressor class."

It took three years to win their case in the Supreme Court by a unanimous vote. The bureaucrats in the Obama administration did not care how bad this looked. "Under the cloak of 'social justice,' the government radicals were determined to prove that their mandates must be obeyed," Horowitz writes.

Horowitz refers to "scores of incidents" of Obama's efforts to stifle religious voices, including using Christmas tree ornaments of Mao Tse-Tung and a drag queen; trying to send pro-abortion ambassadors to the Vatican; institutional intolerance toward any religious beliefs that may negatively affect homosexual "equality;" charging that pro-life advocates are violent criminals; refusing to host the National Day of Prayer and editing "the Creator" out of a reading of the Declaration of Independence.

Obama originally ran on a platform in opposition to same sex marriage. Later, presumably recognizing the campaign support that could be garnered from the gay rights community—he endorsed it and put his weight behind a series of legal cases that led to the June 26, 2015 Supreme Court decision, Obergefell vs. Hodges. The decision overturned a prior Court decision, and requires all states to issue marriage licenses to same-sex couples and to recognize same-sex marriages validly performed in other jurisdictions.

A strong case can be made that Obama's issue switch on the gay marriage topic was not motivated solely by standard political ambition to capture more votes and campaign donations, but rather for the same reason that motivated his career in politics: to "fundamentally transform" America towards socialism and atheistic Marxism.

Subsequently, the Obama administration "was fully behind the gay vigilantes," who harassed Christian bakers, photographers and others for standing by their traditional religious beliefs.

A key feature of all of the recent legislative and legal initiatives in support of "gay rights," health care rights, etc., is the suppression of religious liberty, which Justice Scalia clearly pointed out in his scathing dissent to the Court's overturning of "The Defense of Marriage Act."

Horowitz explains that the Democrat Party has switched its ideological allegiance from Jefferson to Marx, "creating in the process the cavernous divisions in America's political life."

7. Unhinged Attacks

The cultural Marxists who now dominate most of America's major institutions, including the Democrat Party, frame the issues that the media and school teachers then talk about. The dominant issue today is that America is an "Oppressor" nation, says Horowitz. Extreme partisanship is always blamed on the right, never the left. When political leaders like Tom DeLay and Donald Trump refuse to let the left walk all over them, they are charged with bogus illegalities. All of the left's political opponents are labeled as "phobic."

"Stigmatizing one's opponents is a classic radical tactic," says Horowitz, who grew up as a "trained Marxist." He reminds us of Saul Alinsky's statement in his book, *Rules for Radicals*: "Pick the target, freeze it, personalize it, and polarize it." Now it has gotten to the point that anyone who speaks from a place of religious conscience is to be denied his or her First Amendment rights.

Horowitz is a defender of Donald Trump

and his Presidency (the book was published in 2018, so it was written during Trump's first year in office). Trump's defining factor, says Horowitz, is his patriotism, a term that the cultural Marxists, the global elites, and Democrats generally twist into "jingoistic and bigoted bravado."

Traditional, church-going people of faith embraced Trump enthusiastically, says Horowitz, not because they saw in Donald Trump a pious Christian, but because they saw him standing up to the "half century of aggression that religious communities had suffered at the hands of the left...."

The left says this is because evangelical Christians are racists. But Horowitz points out that Evangelicals "were ready to embrace Trump because he cared about America, and the principles behind America's greatness, which are Christian in origin."

This book is explicitly a wake-up call to all church-going, people of faith and fair-minded Americans to better understand the enemy they have been facing for dozens of years—an enemy which has become increasingly successful in achieving their policy goals.

Dark Agenda by David Horowitz will, we hope, alert enough Americans and move them to make a difference. We are in a war for America's very survival as a free, morally responsible nation that recognizes and defends its Christian roots and institutions. The first challenge is to recognize and understand cultural, God-hating, atheistic Marxism for what it is so that we may never again allow ourselves to be deceived.

8. Afterword
By Ross Cleveland
South Central PA Coordinator
Conservative Christian Center

Americans place a lot of reliance on the idea of conscience. Unfortunately, too many don't get the point of this idea: you should make important decisions in your life—such as how to behave, how to treat others, your faith, who you should vote for in elections—with an *informed* conscience. Not just a conscience.

The opposite of that word "informed" would be an uninformed (ignorant) conscience. Or worse, a *malformed* conscience.

Sadly, dear Reader, too many Americans today have an uninformed or malformed conscience. Two examples:

First, those women who kill their babies in the womb. Abortion.

How can a woman kill her own baby? At the least, they are very uninformed if they think that it is not a human being they are killing. Even Aristotle, without the benefit of later science, knew that the seed of a human is not the same thing as the seed of a tree and therefore worthy of protection.

Or at worst, a woman can kill her own baby due to a malformed conscience, such as thinking that their own rights and comfort are the only thing that matters, and they simply do not care that their baby is a human being with its own God-given rights—such as the right to life.

A second example, is when good people of faith, vote in elections, for candidates who are pro-abortion. At best, they have an uninformed (ignorant) conscience. At worst, it is malformed.

Once you realize the truth that David Horowitz writes about in *Dark Agenda: the War to Destroy Christian America*, you no longer have an "uninformed conscience."

If that's true—and I only say this because I fervently believe it is—then you now, after having read this review, only have two choices.

You can, with a malformed conscience, do nothing.

Or you can help us get the word out, about the war to destroy Christian America.

You can help by spreading the word about what you have learned, about this book. You can learn more by reading the book itself, not just this review. You can help by getting more copies of this Review and passing them around to those you know and even to those you meet in the future.

When you vote, make sure it is with an *informed* conscience. That simply means, learn what the candidates stand for on the issues of concern to you. And then vote only for those whose beliefs match your own.

Here in south central Pennsylvania we routinely meet those seeking political office, who want the support of members of our Conservative Christian Center, but won't let us know where they stand on the issues of importance to us. We have published a "Value Voter Guide" for 5 years showing how the candidates answered 10 questions of interest to the faith-based, church-going community.

Incredibly, there are candidates who won't answer any questions at all, or won't answer many of them. "What difference does it make where I stand on the right to life if I am going to be the town Dogcatcher," they explain. We've heard it so often we call it *The Dogcatcher Rule*.

Our belief is that you should only vote for the candidates who best represent your views. Not perfectly. But "best."

How can you do that if the candidate won't tell you what they believe?

So yes, of course, they have the right to remain silent. So does an accused criminal facing a trial But I'm not voting for either one. I urge you to do the same.

Consider how really simple this is. Vote with an informed conscience. How? By knowing where the candidates stand, on the issues important to you. And then, only vote for the candidates, who best represent your beliefs.

If we persuade more church-going, people of faith, to do exactly this and to speak out about their choices, America will be a better place.

I hope you will also lend your support to Conservative Christian Center so that we can distribute more copies of this handy pocketbook. Get more copies and give them out. Help us.

If you don't help, then the bad people with

their dreadful, anti-Christian, anti-America philosophy, will not only win elections and run the country—but they will implement their *Dark Agenda*. The choice is yours.

Thank you for reading this and God bless you, your family and our country.

From the desk of
Former Rep. Gary Giordano

Dear friend,

If we can get one million copies of this paperback out to church-going people of faith I believe it will energize a backlash against those working to destroy the America of our founders.

<u>Will you help</u>? Please do your part.

First, order more pocketbooks and give them out. Second, buy the actual *Dark Agenda* book.

And finally, give a donation to Conservative Christian Center.

With your help we can stop America from turning into a Marxist wasteland. Try to send $25 or more. Thank you and God bless you.

Sincerely,

Former State Rep. Gary Giordano

How to Donate:
Make check payable and mail to:
Christian Conservative Center
Freedom Center Fulfilment Dept.
P.O. Box 820
Stuarts Draft, Virginia 24477-0820
Or www.ConservativeChristianCenter.org

About Former Representative Gary Giordano

Gary Giordano, Executive Director of White House Watch Fund (formerly White House Defense Fund under President Trump), is a former State Representative in Arizona (1985–1989), married with 5 children and 6 grandchildren and a licensed Arizona Hunting guide, registered Representative and Insurance Agent.

Gary Giordano is a lifetime conservative, starting with Young Americans for Freedom as a chapter, regional and state chairman before being appointed to the National HQ Staff. He is a founding member of the independent YAF Archive, the listserv for and by YAF senior alumni.

About Professor Kevin Peterson, Major, USAF (Retired)
Project Director, Conservative Christian Center

Professor Kevin Peterson, Major, USAF (Retired) is the Project Director of Conservative Christian Center (CCC). A Virginia resident, he has traveled to Pennsylvania on numerous occasions to speak at and help the local CCC clubs in Cumberland and York County. He has for eight years been a national director of United States Public Policy Council, the parent organization of CCC and is now spearheading the national CCC program.

Since his college years, Kevin has served the Church in various volunteer roles including worship leader, teacher, youth advisor and leadership council member. He's also been active in movements to encourage mainstream denominations to remain faithful to Biblical principles and worldview despite pressure to "evolve" and conform to liberal social precepts.

Kevin completed a career in the US Air Force

where he served as a scientific and technical intelligence engineer, counterintelligence analyst, investigator and crime analyst covering issues such as workplace violence, drug crimes, trans-national terrorism and intellectual property theft affecting military readiness.

Since retiring, he has served in several security-related positions within the defense industry and launched an independent consulting practice focused on security risk management and training. For over 20 years, Kevin has been an adjunct professor of graduate studies in security management, teaching in the classroom and online for two universities that primarily serve adult learners and mid-career professionals.

Kevin is also a contributing author to books and publications on a variety of topics including security risk management, investigations, information protection, threat analysis, security careers and security in houses of worship. He holds a bachelor's degree in engineering and a master's in systems management.

The simple paperback that's paving the way for an "America First" comeback in 2022 and 2024—maybe even with President Donald Trump himself!

What can you do to pave the way for "America First" conservatives to win back the House and Senate in 2022 and then the White House in 2024, **maybe even with Donald Trump himself**? It starts with ordering your copy of the new paperback, *A Review of the Book The Case for Trump by Victor Davis Hanson*.

Arm yourself with the facts you need to defend Donald Trump by picking up your copy today. Or get multiple copies and distribute them to open-minded Americans you know to help us lay the groundwork for an "America First" comeback in 2022 and 2024.

How to Order:

1 copy = $5	3 copies = $10
10 copies = $25	100 copies = $150

Please include a postage and handling fee of $3 plus 10% and make your check payable to and mail to:

Christian Conservative Center:
Freedom Center Fulfilment Dept.
P.O. Box 820, Stuarts Draft, Virginia 24477-0820
Or **www.ConservativeChristianCenter.org**

They laughed when I said no, Donald Trump was not responsible for the COVID-19 virus. But when I gave them this little paperback…

Liberals desperately want Americans to believe Donald Trump was responsible for COVID-19. They want Joe Biden to get the credit for Donald Trump's successful vaccine rollout, and, more than anything, they want to stop a Trump comeback in 2024.

But this paperback exposes their **Big Lies** and tells the truth about how Donald Trump saved millions of lives.

This paperback will give you the facts you need to wipe the smirks off the faces of the Liberals who blame Donald Trump for COVID-19. Or take it a step further and help us share the truth with open-minded Americans to stop the spread of their Big Lies.

How to Order:

1 copy = $5   3 copies = $10
10 copies = $25   100 copies = $150

Please include a postage and handling fee of $3 plus 10% and make your check payable to and mail to:

Christian Conservative Center:
Freedom Center Fulfilment Dept.
P.O. Box 820, Stuarts Draft, Virginia 24477-0820
Or **www.ConservativeChristianCenter.org**

Don't miss your chance to own the new publication with the power to <u>crush socialism in America</u>—a conservative must-have for the Biden era!

It's a fact: right now, **socialism is winning** and, and **conservatism is losing**. But this new paperback, *A Review of the Book United States of Socialism by Dinesh D'Souza*, helps conservatives rally everyday Americans against Biden-backed Marxism and preserve the founding principles of our country.

Not only does this paperback equip you with all the arguments you need to expose your friends, relatives, and co-workers to the evil truths of socialism, but, even better, you can order extra copies and gift them to open-minded Americans, so they too join the fight to ensure our Republic withstands the Biden era and elect "America First" conservatives in 2022 and 2024!

How to Order:

1 copy = $5	3 copies = $10
10 copies = $25	100 copies = $150

Please include a postage and handling fee of $3 plus 10% and make your check payable to and mail to:

Christian Conservative Center:
Freedom Center Fulfilment Dept.
P.O. Box 820, Stuarts Draft, Virginia 24477-0820
Or **www.ConservativeChristianCenter.org**

How do we turn the tide in the war to destroy Christian America? The answer is in this new paperback…

Radical Marxists are working to dismantle, dislodge, and destroy Christian America. Who are these people and why are they succeeding?

Because too many conservative Christians have turned away from the political process, refusing to register, speak out, campaign for their beliefs, or even vote.

This new paperback, *A Review of the Book Dark Agenda: The War to Destroy Christian America by David Horowitz*, is **the wake-up call Christian America needs.** It tells you how to mobilize and energize people in your church or faith community. Order extra copies to share with Christians you know to ensure Americans of faith flock to the polls in droves in 2022, 2024, and beyond!

How to Order:

1 copy = $5	3 copies = $10
10 copies = $25	100 copies = $150

Please include a postage and handling fee of $3 plus 10% and make your check payable to and mail to:

Christian Conservative Center:
Freedom Center Fulfilment Dept.
P.O. Box 820, Stuarts Draft, Virginia 24477-0820
Or **www.ConservativeChristianCenter.org**